C000142030

A PICTORIAL PARADE OF
SOUTHERN REGION ROAD VEHICLES

Bruce Murray & Kevin Robertson

ISBN 978-1-906419-29-5

First published in 2009 by Kevin Robertson under the **NOODLE BOOKS** imprint
PO Box 279 Corhampton, SOUTHAMPTON SO32 3ZX

www.kevinrobertsonbooks.co.uk

Printed in England by Ian Allan Printing Ltd.

Authors note; we would like to express our thanks to former Road Vehicle Inspector,
Fred Emery, without whose help this work could not have been compiled.

Front cover - Ford 5-ton diesel-engined van, 1144S, with a Tilt canopy. Tilt canopy body designs were fairly unusual on cartage fleet vehicles, so this one may have been for the Service Department fleet: despite having a cartage style fleet number. The vehicle has rubber front wings, which were an attempt to avoid accident damage. In service, the rubber quickly became hard and consequently brittle. At least one vehicle of this type was repaired, and subsequently sported one rubber and one replacement metal wing. Believed taken at Brighton Goods, 4 February 1957.

Frontispiece - A posed load of crates and general cartage in the rear of a rigid vehicle. Trunks, boxes with straw packing and the general use of string, are all indicative of the period, in what was the pre-polystyrene and brown tape era. Nine Elms Goods, 17 February 1955. (See views page 35).

Rear cover - A Scammell tractor unit and associated trailers in the yard at Crawley. The workaday condition of the vehicles is all too obvious, as indeed is the state of the concrete posts on the edge of the platform. Notice too the pile of wicker baskets in the background.

Paul Hersey collection

INTRODUCTION

The subject of the Road Vehicles from the British Railways era is one which has received only limited book and magazine coverage in recent years. Indeed it is perhaps somewhat ironic that the vehicles operated by the pre-group and pre-nationalisation companies are still recorded in far greater detail. (GW Road Vehicles / LMS Road Vehicles / Railway Bus Services - all published by OPC some years ago).

It would be very nice then to be able to accurately state that at last we might put the record straight, with a full record, description of every type and fleet / registration numbers for the BR period. Unfortunately that cannot be the case for the present work. Consequently we must apologise that whilst what follows is as comprehensive a volume as we have been able to amass, such detail as we have included can only be part of the story: but we hope still a very attractive and valuable part. Despite searching for and enquiries over, a fleet record / register of road vehicles operated by the Southern Region has still not be uncovered. (If it is out there somewhere we would love to see it, perhaps even complete this record with publication in 'Southern Way').

The photographs and notes that follow were compiled by former Road Vehicle Inspector, Fred Emery. Not only a career railwayman, but a lifelong enthusiast as well. I have had the pleasure of knowing Fred for some years, which resulted, soon after the start of the 'Southern Way' series, in Fred passing to me a large envelope of black and white images of railway road vehicles, nearly all from what is his favourite Southern Region. Add to this notes from Fred's meticulous memory and the result is what is now reproduced here.

The actual photographs had been discarded as irrelevant and were to be dumped in a skip ready for disposal. We can only imagine what other goodies might have been similarly thrown away. Fred's experiences in this are no more than occurred at countless other locations and reference countless other subjects. Material now of invaluable use, both to the enthusiast and from an historical perspective, was discarded as unwanted: yesterdays news. To be fair the railway probably had little option. Government charged the railway with operating a service, not spending resources on the retention and storage of old paperwork.

But even if what we see here is just the tip of the proverbial ice-berg, what a veritable feast it still presents. A glimpse into a part of what was the overall operation of the railway, a time when countless wayside yards were served by countless trains, the goods to and from which were received and despatched by railway lorry. All too often it has been the express train and locomotive that has been the centre of attention, in this book there is not a single view of a railway engine.

Instead what we have are the everyday scenes, as well as the 'official' type views no doubt recorded when the vehicles were new. Wherever possible we have selected images that portray background as well, whilst others have been chosen as they represent the best of a small but otherwise similar batch. - how many views of a Scammell badge would you like!

To set the scene, we have adopted a deliberate approach. The first is by the inclusion of Fred's own introductory notes. These are followed by the few views in the collection that record actual Southern Railway as opposed to Southern Region scenes. In this early part it will quickly be noted that not all the vehicles are lettered 'SR', but there is a deliberate reason for this, and which is the general carrier status whereby vehicles operated by a number of other organisations might well also deliver and collect goods, sometimes 'own account' to and from the railway. These contemporary illustrations are worth including for their general interest alone.

We do hope you approve, the whole compilation having given us both a welcome diversion from the more usual railway album.

Kevin Robertson and Bruce Murray

The Photographic Record - comments by Fred Emery

"Most of the illustrations seen in this book are from official views taken by the Southern Region of British railways in the period up to about 1961. The scenes were recorded in connection with a project regarding road vehicles but the subsequent formation of National Carriers (NCL) meant both the vehicles and photographs were unwanted, specific NCL vehicles to be used from then on.

The view seen represent only some of the enormous variety of lorries, (rigid, drawbar, tractor-units and associated trailers) used by the railway. It will also be noted that virtually all are cartage vehicles and not service vehicles. In fact during the period the views were taken there were still comparatively few vehicles in the 'service departments': when I joined the railway in the mid 1960s, the SR had around 60 actual service vehicles, yet by the 1980s there were over 1,100, mainly small vans including a large quantity on long term hire.

It was also the practice that if a department, CME, Signalling etc, wanted a vehicle, they would borrow one from the cartage fleet often with a cartage section driver. Numbering of the vehicle fleet changed significantly over the years. To commence with there was just a simple numbering system, such as '18S', the letter indicating 'Southern Region'. At a later time, (date unknown), the numbering was given a prefix to more accurately represent the actual vehicle. Thus 7T 3019 S was a 7-ton Ford followed by a fleet number and again the owning region. To add to the confusion the letter 'M' after the number could also represent 'Road Motor' and was a simple continuation of former Southern Railway practice but was later dropped to avoid the obvious confusion with the London Midland Region fleet."

A 6-ton Scammell mechanical horse and trailer post war and possibly in the Kent area. We cannot be certain if the delivery (collection?) was being made to Boots, International Stores (who were offering 'Margarine Reduced In Price') or elsewhere, although it will be noted wooden crates were the norm. This was long before the days of the electric tail-lifts. The protrusions above the bonnet on either side are the side lights, although the illumination from these was sadly restricted. Also, protruding from the bonnet on the driver's side is the horn. The cast plate on the front, besides proclaiming the name of the manufacturer, incorporated the vehicle capacity, three or six ton type.

Milepost 92½ Picture Library

A 3- ton Scammell Mechanical Horse, brand new in Watford, the town of manufacture and posed outside the Isolation Hospital. These vehicles had a single piece of glass across the windscreen which opened horizontally. The small splasher (mudguard) over the front wheel appears to be painted in this view, although other photographs would imply this was sometimes a different colour to the bodywork or was even left unpainted. Notice the top of the doors were open with no weather protection. The circular holder is for the road fund licence, two further holders later being added for the respective carrier licences for the vehicle and trailer - these are shown in a different position on the larger capacity vehicle opposite. On the vehicle seen above the chassis members and wheel centres appear to be black, compared with what was then the official colour of red for these parts.

Opposite page - Part of a series of official Scammell views depicting the coupling and uncoupling process of a vehicle and trailer - this one has a red painted chassis as well. The driver is most certainly not a railway employee, witness the Brylcreem hair, gauntlets and spotted cravat. **Above** - A 6-ton Mechanical-Horse, post war, and at an unreported location. Unusually, compared with the view on page 4, this vehicle does not appear to sport a headlight. The lack of a nearside mirror is interesting, some drivers would fit these themselves but they rarely remained in situ long before being 'borrowed'. Later such an essential fitment became a legal requirement. The letters R T on the trailer may indicate 'Rail Transfer' and applied to movements between London stations. The dents on the bodywork were a typical workaday feature.

Whilst not immediately obvious as a railway road vehicle, the Hay's Wharf Cartage Company Ltd. was 100% owned by the four pre-nationalisation railways, each having a 25% share. After 1 January 1948 however, instead of working alongside the railway it became a competitor overnight, passing not to the nationalised British Railways but instead to the British Road Services / Pickfords organisation. On this page a 6-ton Scammell is seen at what may well be a railhead. Opposite a collection / delivery is being made again at an unknown location, but with a distinct docklands feel.

The versatility of the articulated vehicle is seen to advantage here. Notice also what are 6 - ton Scammells, have been fitted with a split windscreen by this time. Again the locations are not given but from the detail of the For Sale board in the right hand view, by implication it is in the EC2 area. Seen from above in what was clearly a posed picture, the bed of the trailers are depicted as clean and well swept, in practice a rare occurrence, leading to debris of all sorts bouncing off onto the road surface to play havoc with the tyres of following traffic. The Scammell coupling in use here incorporated an automatic contact connection for the rear lights, although in practice this was very much a hit or miss affair, especially as the equipment aged. The rear numberplate for the trailer was the responsibility of the driver, but was often forgotten.

Above - Flat trailer 6184 M-S with the handbrake picked out in white. This was a fairly standard type of trailer, the headboard of which could be removed to leave a completely flat load area. A tailboard could also be fitted which could be removed, or lowered. In later years when wheeled trolley containers were a regular load, this type of trailer having a low front headboard, could cause problems with loads tipping and falling into the gap between the semi-trailer and drawing unit. 8 February 1952.

Opposite page - 4093M, a Scammell Scarab 3 - ton petrol engine unit. (The 3 - ton vehicles were originally all petrol engined but the larger 6 - ton variant was usually diesel). By this time, 8 February 1952, the railway were also using a considerable number of manufacturers 'off the peg' designs. It is believed the views were respectively recorded at East Croydon and Brighton Goods.

Opposite page - 3-ton capacity box trailer with shutter at rear, (these would often jam if the runners became damaged - a regular occurrence). A fairly conventional trailer but seen here with the roof panel painted over , later bodies had the centre of the fibreglass roof panel left translucent in lieu of any form of internal light. Advertising, both railway and as here seen here commercial, was a regular feature. Photographed at Preston Park, Brighton, 8 March 1956.

Above - Similar to that seen opposite except this trailer was fitted with rear curtains. As with the back of rigid vehicles, it appeared the railway could not make up their mind which type of fitting to standardise upon. This particular trailer was designated for use at Deptford but was photographed at Bricklayers Arms on 5 March 1956.

Recorded near Battersea Park on 4 June 1954, was this 3-ton Scammell Scarab petrol engine tractor attached to a tipping trailer, both from the Service Department: Chief Civil Engineers fleet. Although the standard livery is applied to the tractor unit, the trailer appears to be in a lighter shade: green perhaps? Whilst the normal tractor and trailer coupling in use at that time, (official known as a 'Scammell' coupling), meant it was possible to attach and detach a conventional trailer without the driver leaving his cab, he would still be responsible for applying / releasing the trailer handbrake, checking the lights, and fitting / removing the rear number plate. (On some of the early Scammells there was a slot for this to be placed on the outside rear of the cab - it was often forgotten). In this example it was also necessary to disconnect the hydraulic pipe from the tipping mechanism, the tank and connection for which, can be seen on the nearside of the unit. Side windows have also now been fitted to this model of vehicle.

Above - Rear view of a 3–ton trailer in East Croydon Goods Yard, 8 February 1952. The small removable tail board can be seen. Of interest is the single rear light above the number plate and of limited use on the road. Some of the debris spoken of earlier which applied to semi-trailers, can be seen. **Opposite page** - A 2-ton Morrison 'Electricar' in East Croydon Goods Yard, 17 November 1950. These were tried experimentally but a combination of restricted haulage capacity, inefficient battery operation, the extra weight of the batteries, and consequently a limited range of useful activity, meant they failed to find favour. Even so visually at least two different types were tried, which might mean there were technical as well as aesthetic differences. The registration number is not from a sequence normally associated with BR vehicles.

Opposite page - A standard 3-ton box trailer recorded in the early 1950s. Although not visible in this view are the three windows fitted to this type of curved roof trailer and again intended to afford some degree of internal illumination. Neither the location nor the meaning of the letters P and T are recorded.

Above - A trailer from the same batch but seen here at East Croydon attached to an 'Electricar'. It cannot be confirmed if this was the same Morrison vehicle depicted previously, as in this view there is no fleet number present. Notice also the accident damage present on the nearside wing. The use of four wheels on the tractor units, compared with the 3-wheel Scammell / Karrier type, did increase stability but at the expense of manoeuvrability.

A possible earlier type of Morrison vehicle seen above left, in East Croydon Yard, no doubt shortly after delivery. (The registration number has yet to be added). For sole running the same pathetic rear light is fitted. **Above Right** - A 6-ton box trailer this time with the variant of two end windows and central ventilator. The plate referring to the letters 'DE' is again unexplained). Notice that at this both the rear of the tractor units and also the trailers only had a single wheel on either side. The metal supporting wheels on the front of the trailer were also wont to sink into soft ground on occasions. This could be corrected at the time of uncoupling by having a plank of wood underneath although should the trailer be too low or too high in relation to the unit then re-coupling became difficult if not impossible. 2 March 1950.**Opposite page** - By now licenced for the road as NGX 222 and photographed at Battersea Park on 11 May 1954. Interestingly this design of vehicle would appear to be to an older style compared with that photographed four years previously.

Above - A 6-ton trailer with drop down tail board and shutter. No steps were provided for the driver to surmount the trailer itself and he was expected to climb up and jump down as necessary. Slightly unusually also there is no provision for advertising, perhaps these were added later. Location unknown, 2 March 1950. **Opposite page** - Another electric vehicle, consecutively numbered with that seen earlier so far as the fleet number is concerned but still to receive a registration number. The single wiper and mirror on the offside will be noted. Only one seat was provided in most railway vehicles of this era, both articulated and rigid, should a 'mate' be required then it was practice to purloin a suitable box or parcel as a temporary refuge. East Croydon, 16 January 1952.

Above - A 6-ton flat trailer with front gantry / headboard of the style very much used by the railway. The location is Redhill (Earlswood) goods yard on 8 April 1957.
Opposite page - What appears at first glance to be a standard 6-ton Commer QX petrol engine vehicle - the give away to the latter is the starting handle, although even so this must have been a real brute to turn over by hand. Externally then a conventional cartage vehicle, but which is in fact a bullion van, the attendants for which would be confined in the claustrophobic fashion seen. One driver recalled how on one occasion he transported £250,000 in sacks of coin in a standard cartage trailer. The views were recorded at Battersea Wharf with part of Chelsea Bridge just visible in the background. 11 November 1953.

BRITISH RAILWAYS

501
S

NUW 828

Opposite page - A Ford ED6 diesel-engined van recorded at Brighton when new on 8 May 1956, it was unlikely to remain in such pristine condition for long. The small window behind the driver were not ideal if required for reversing - see also next page. Reasonable lighting, wipers for both windows, two mirrors and two seats are though provided. **Above -** The same style of mechanics but with a smaller 2-ton capacity. Metal front wings, painted black are fitted, whilst the body having an arced top displays a much older appearance. (Were the bodies in fact re-used?) Only one wiper is fitted on this vehicle although both vehicles have an opening windscreen ahead of the driver. Brighton, 11 October 1955.

Rear views of the vehicle seen on the previous page. Both are fitted with roll-type shutters, whilst careful examinations will reveal that whilst PYO 567 displayed two small windows behind the driver when viewed from the front, only one could be used for rearward observation. The earlier comment of possible re-use of old bodywork might also be considered again as witness the position of the rear lights. Those on PYO 496 are chassis mounted off the bodywork, due to the width of the tailboard, whilst its neighbour has lighting incorporated into the bodywork. Even so on the former the lights would be totally obscured when the tailboard was lowered. This no doubt led to accidents as in later days openings were cut into the tailboard to correspond with the lights being seen. As with the alterations at the front, so two rear lights are also provided. Location and dates as before. All BR road vehicles were allocated on paper an allotted life. Should however one be written off during that time span then the accountancy system then in use dictated a similar vehicle had to hired for the balance of the presumed life. No early purchase replacement was permitted. It made for considerable extra cost for the railway, although was no doubt very profitable to the hire companies involved!

A 2-ton Ford, similar in style to that seen earlier but this time with rubber front wings, again the same comments as before apply. On the plus side these Fords were recalled as being both reliable and speedy but were quite noisy to drive. At the front there is what appears to be an unofficial radiator blind, (perhaps unusual that is was allowed to remain in situ for the photographer), whilst at the rear the handle to assist in climbing may also be another unofficial adornment. The rear curtains were afford a degree of weather protection to the load but limited security. That said it was common practice also for keys to left in the ignition or if the latter item had been lost for a screwdriver or similar permanently wedged in the switch. As will be gathered, where possible drivers were allocated the same vehicle. The metal plate on the tailboard (indicated with the arrow), had on the opposite side a rudimentary step to allow ease of access. Recorded at Battersea Wharf. 5 June 1956.

RYX 763 was a 5 ton Ford ED6 diesel, fitted with a canopy tilt body and having rubber front wings: the rear mudguards though are metal. Notice the spare wheel, in practice these were either removed or they would disappear: as would batteries and on occasions the fuel from the tanks. The fold in the canopy can be explained one of two ways, either it has simply not be pulled taut, or as appears more likely, the metal supporting frame did not extend to the rear of the body. (Could this even be the reason this series of views was taken?) At this time, 27 April 1956, a 20 mph speed limit still applied to commercial vehicles of unladen weight above 3 tons, so the '20' plate on the rear would appear to be an incorrect fixing. (The 20 limit for vehicles above 3 tons was raised to 30 shortly afterwards). Views taken at Brighton Goods.

RAILWAY CARTAGE

2 37
S

DIESEL

Slightly unusual in that the views on these pages show a British Road Services vehicle transferred to British Railways. The vehicle is an Austin (BMC) diesel van, under 3-ton capacity. Notice on the rear the painted out BRS fleet number although the original owner designation still appears at the front. Livery is in what is believed to be dark green and black. The load is probably posed but was still typical of the period. As can be gauged from the side, the wheel arches protrude into the bodywork and could be a real nuisance with some loads. Believed to be taken at Clapham Common, 18 June 1956.

An Austin 'Loadstar' 2-ton capacity fitted with a petrol engine. Recalled as speedy, no doubt due to the type of engine fitted, and also quite reliable. Vehicles of this type, but with variations in the type of bodywork, were supplied to numerous organisations including the Armed Forces. Interestingly it appears twin wheels on the rear became standard earlier on rigid vehicles compared with their articulated equivalent. This particular vehicle was certainly not photographed when new, although any marks and grime would appear to be as per normal workaday wear and tear. Interesting the mud flaps only apply to the front wheels. It was recalled that the drivers seat on these vehicles consisted of a cushion held by a form of tab onto a metal box. The box itself securely attached to the bodywork and used for storing tools etc. The seat back was also securely attached to the same box. The weak point though was the cushion and which could detach itself without warning thus making for an unnerving experience for the driver. Location unknown, 6 April 1954.

Opposite page - A 6/8 ton flat trailer with drop frame. The variation in carrying capacity was dependent upon the towing unit. This type of trailer was used for cable drums and also containers where low headroom at the destination prevented a normal height trailer being used. The picked out areas of white were not just for the benefit of the camera, all 6-ton trailers were originally identified in this way and intended to remind the driver that it could only be coupled to the correct type of tractor unit: but see also page 43 where the white paint has almost totally disappeared. East Croydon, 16 February 1955. **Above** - An Austin 8-ton forward-control diesel engine tractor unit. (Forward-control referred to the fact the driver sat either on top of or ahead of the front axle and as such the steering and foot pedal passed through a linkage backwards). Recalled as reliable but rust later became a major problem in the thin metalwork used for the cab. Battersea Wharf, 7 August 1956.

Above - A specific use trailer, not as might first be imagined for livestock, but instead for the movement of sheet glass. Officially a 3-ton 'glass-float' trailer, it would also used for loads of similar type, sheet metal and plywood for example. (It might be expected the maximum capacity could also be reached fairly quickly). Notice the clamps inside the vehicle for keeping the load secure and upright. As might have been expected, there is no rear tailboard. 29 March 1955 and possibly at Southampton.

Opposite page - A Karrier Bantam, 3-ton petrol engine unit. Believed photographed in 1957, by which time the 'M' suffix to the fleet number had been dropped. These units were noticeably under-powered and unstable in poor weather when being driven 'solo. This applied particularly to the diesel engine version where there was a greater weight on the front axle. The view is believed taken in the Brighton / Worthing area.

Opposite page - An Austin 8-ton normal control diesel unit at Battersea Wharf on 4 February 1957. The cab and bonnet structure of these lorries was sprung separately from the chassis consequently there was some 'joy' in store for the driver when running 'solo' (- meaning without a trailer attached), until he became used to their behaviour. Notice the position of the spare wheel, ideal for storing ropes and chains. **Above** - A 6/8 ton trailer of similar type to that seen before but included due to the location, Fratton Goods Depot and the presence of 1242S, a Bedford 'O' in the background. It is likely the latter is in departmental service, probably carrying green livery. This particular yard was shared with British Road Services and eventually became an NCL depot in 1968. Photographed on 5 April 1957.

Above - Brighton Goods Yard on 13 February 1955 with an 8-ton 'Pole trailer in the foreground. Also known as a 'trombone', these trailers were extendable to cater for longer loads. The secondary 'jockey' wheels were insurance when a loaded trailer was being attached or detached to the towing vehicle, as the automatic Scammell coupling did not at the time include 'limited collapse' on the undercarriage. Two other road vehicles can also be identified, in the distance an electric 'internal movement' vehicle - see pages 60 to 63, whilst to the left is a departmental Bedford 'A' dropside lorry. The rake of fish vans would probably have arrived full and been unloaded, rather than awaiting a load caught off the south coast. **Opposite page** - The first of the 4-wheel tractor units, an Austin 6-ton petrol vehicle. Although popular with the drivers, they were recalled as having a trait whereby the driver's seat would collapse without warning. Photographed in Nine Elms Goods Yard. 9 April 1954.

Opposite page - A 3-ton box trailer with side shutters: presumably on both sides, possibly one of a batch built for a specific task as the length is greater than usual. The twin doors at the rear were another most unusual (for the Southern Region) feature. This type of door could cause trouble when opened in high winds. This trailer was maker to work only with 'Karrier Bantam' units, see page 40, and would appear to have similar size road wheels. Photographed, it is believed, at East Croydon on 11 June 1956. In this as in several views within this album, it will be noted the recommended tyre pressure was often painted above the wheel concerned. **Above** - A 10-ton low headboard flat trailer recorded at Battersea Wharf on 26 July 1954. The bridge in the background carries the main lines in and out of Victoria.

A 'meaty' (the word is used deliberately for reasons that will become apparent) 6-ton Leyland Beaver and very modern for its time. The flatbed loading area was ideal for carrying two 'AF' type containers of meat, which would be taken, along with a drawbar trailer carrying a similar load, from the railway yards to the various meat markets. Some customers who did not have a crane facility would have the containers arrive on the lorry sideways on, and meaning both sets of container doors would be accessible from the side to allow for ease of loading / unloading. Although designated 6-ton, they often carried loads in excess of 8-tons. The views were recorded in Nine Elms Goods Yard, 19 July 1951. The framework at the font was so that the vehicle might be turned around and attached to the trailer to push the latter to its required unloading point.

Opposite page - An identical type vehicle to that seen on the previous page but with a posed load of fruit boxes. The picture was recorded for effect only, as the complete load shown here would have been unlikely to have exceeded much over one ton in weight and consequently was wasteful use of a powerful vehicle. Note the tool box on the nearside, used for stowage of necessary securing items. Roping was also the standard practice at this time, as indeed it still was on railway wagons, the roping and sheeting of a lorry load nowadays an almost forgotten art. Nine Elms Goods Yard, 15 March 1951. **Above** - Drawbar trailer 2484M at Nine Elms Goods and of the type that would be hauled by the Leyland seen opposite. This type of trailer varied with either metal or rubber wings over the rear axle wheels.

Above - A 6-ton capacity drawbar trailer seen in the goods yard at Nine Elms. Notice the cable visible at the front, this was a rudimentary brake for the trailer which was attached to a simple brake lever in the cab and operated by the drivers 'mate' - the latter a legal requirement on all vehicles with a trailer. The (in)efficiency of the system is perhaps best left to the imagination. In the background is a Thorneycroft, which apart from the BR logo, appears to still retain SR livery. **Opposite page** - A 3-ton Cattle Float trailer, already by the time of the photograph, 1952, unlikely to be seeing much use. This type of trailer was also used for transporting railway horses when necessary.

53

Both pages - OYL 461 was a 6-ton Sentinal rigid lorry, photographed at Nine Elms Goods on 17 February 1955. Referred to sometimes as a 'Leyland Sentinal' by BR. They were unusual in that the engine was mounted under the floor behind the cab: similar in many respects to where the boiler of the earlier Sentinal steam-lorry had been fitted. Why they were purchased in the first place is not certain, possibly a BTC requirement that orders had to be split around different manufacturers or perhaps the original choice could not supply at the time. (That is not to suggest theses vehicles were in any way inferior.) Some of the other BR regions also came to possess similar vehicles around the same time. Notice also the sliding doors provided, tiny wing mirrors and what was a posed load of crates. Again the hook for manoeuvring a trailer from the front is prominent.

Opposite page - A 15-ton multi-wheel trailer used for specialist loads: the destination on this occasion was London Airport with the trailer photographed at Nine Elms. At this time, 1951, it was still amazing what type of loads British railways carried - some of which must have made Pickfords a bit hot under the collar.

Above - A 15-ton pole trailer, the rear axle of which could be set at different positions along the chassis. The view is believed to have been taken at Bricklayers Arms in December 1954. Notice in the background the covered van pushed hard up against the buffers, lettered J S Fry and Sons, of Keynsham, and specifically marked, 'Shunt With Great Care' as its usual load would be chocolate biscuits and confectionary.

Both pages - Trailer 2389M again but this time in its unloaded state. It is tempting to suggest the load seen earlier has was being delivered to the Airport rather than being collected, but we cannot be certain. (One end of the tank barrel seen earlier referred to Las Palmas.) The background scenes in these two views show just how much ahs changed over the years whilst just visible also is the drawing locomotive (Road Traffic Act definition that is 'Light Locomotive' or 'Heavy Locomotive' according to weight), used to haul the trailer.

Pages 60, 61, 62 and 63 - Scammell electric-powered internal movement units and associated trailer, all depicted in the streets outside Brighton Goods Yard on 5 May 1953. Numbered S360S for the tractor unit and ST138 for the trailer, this was one of several conversions made from elderly petrol mechanical horses to electric powered vehicles for internal shunting and movement: note the photographs though were taken on the public road! Similar vehicles existed at a number of large yards, whose purpose was to move goods from wagons to depot loading banks, and vice versa, or transfer goods between wagons. The conversions (presumably undertaken by Scammell?), involved removal of the former petrol engine and also a substitute one-man cab. Colour scheme was an overall grey and they were then specifically identified as to their

Continued page 62 /-

From page 60 / - internal or depot use only. The colour scheme, plus the associated ancestry of a 'mechanical-horse', quickly gave rise to the soubriquet of 'The Old Grey Mares' or 'Dolly Greys' - the latter a sop towards a supposed racehorse. Another, perhaps slightly less flattering term was that of a 'pram'. Being internal maintenance vehicles they were subject to countless knocks and crunches whilst also only receiving limited maintenance. As such more were usually found dumped as unserviceable in odd corners of a yard. The trailer covering would appear to be almost a home-made affair and afforded only arbitery protection against the elements. The vehicle was thus unlikely to remain in the almost pristine condition seen for very long. In time such vehicles were replaced by conventional vehicles withdrawn from normal traffic, but which retained conventional livery.

Recorded at an unknown location, a brand new Scammell is seen amongst a background of two other vehicles including an earlier SR liveried mechanical horse. The date is 22 March 1950 and the colour scheme to the rear of the cab may well have been all over maroon. As before, the letters 'D E' are unreported. The vehicle gives the impression as having recently been overhauled at a workshop. So far as the Southern Region was concerned there were several such facilities, including Brighton, Bournemouth and Battersea: the latter in the former roundhouse.

London: Her
Majesty's
Stationery
Office

Henry VIII
and the Development of
Coastal
Defence

B.M.Morley
Inspector of
Ancient Monuments

Department
of the
Environment

Ancient
Monuments
and Historic
Buildings

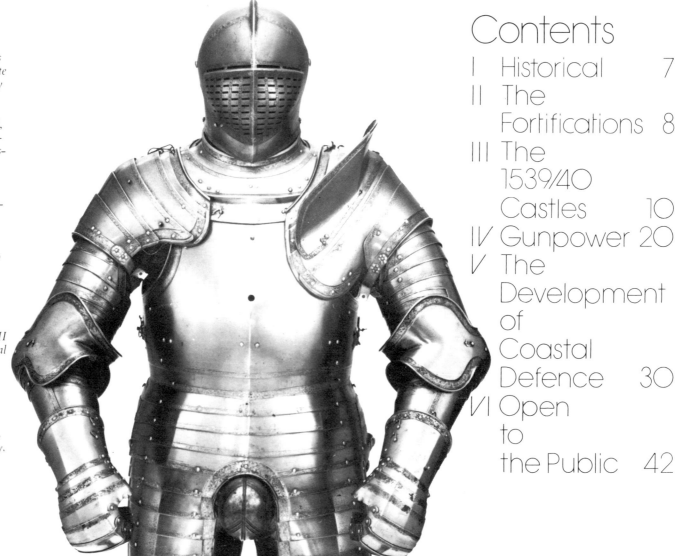

Colour Frontis-piece: 'The Castles in the Downs', a late seventeenth-century painting of the east Kent castles – Walmer, Deal, and, in the distance, Sandown (Walmer Castle, Crown copyright). Title page: Early cannon, from a book of 1511 (British Museum). This page: Suit of armour made for Henry VIII in 1540 at the royal workshops, Greenwich (Tower of London armouries, Crown copyright). Page 5: Henry VIII by Holbein (National Portrait Gallery).

Book designed by Peter Forster, DOE

Printed in England for Her Majesty's Stationery Office by Martin Cadbury, Worcester.
Dd 290325 K412 9/76

Contents

Historical

Henry VIII was an ambitious man, both for himself and his country. The England he inherited in 1509 was very much a minor country in a Europe dominated by France, Spain and the Holy Roman Empire. From the very start of his reign he involved himself in the politics of Europe by flamboyant diplomacy backed up by campaigns of war. These, though not always successful, were always expensive and quickly drained the treasury left by his father. Henry's first success was in the war with France in 1512–1514, which enabled him to bargain with her king, Francis I, on equal terms. In 1519 Charles V of Spain, nephew of Henry's wife, Catherine of Aragon, was elected Emperor, thus securing control of the major part of Europe. Henry joined with him in 1522 in a further drive against France. Initially this had little success, but Francis was at last defeated by the Emperor at the Battle of Pavia in 1525. If Charles were to take France, he would have virtual control of the whole of Europe. Rather than see this, Henry decided to switch allegiance and make his peace with France, although this time under Francis's

conditions. The Pope similarly backed France, but the cost for him was heavy: in 1527 the Emperor's army sacked Rome. Francis set out for Italy, with financial support from Henry, but the campaign was a disaster and England was left almost bankrupt.

At this time Henry had been married to Catherine for 18 years, but had no son. He now wished to divorce her in order to marry a younger woman, Anne Boleyn. Only the Pope had power to grant this but he was now politically subject to Charles, Henry's enemy, and nephew to Catherine. The matter dragged on for six years and ultimately was only solved by Henry's breaking with the Church of Rome and setting himself up as supreme head of the Church in England. At home this sparked off an anti-clerical revolution which gave Henry the opportunity to win favour with his people and to refill the Royal coffers at the same time by dissolving the monasteries and redistributing their lands and wealth. Abroad it hardened the Pope's growing resolve to unite France and the Empire against England. By diplomatic means Henry endeavoured to keep them apart, but in 1538 they signed a ten-year truce and an invasion to re-establish the

Pope's authority in England seemed inevitable.

England was ill prepared for invasion, but Henry acted quickly. Musters were held and he assembled his fleet, such as it was, at Portsmouth. In addition he appointed Commissioners to 'search and defend' the coastline. His intention was to have a chain of forts and batteries around the island to protect access to the major ports and to prevent an enemy invasion fleet from making use of the principal anchorages and landing places. Very few such works existed already. There had been a few small blockhouses built in the South and South West during the earlier French wars. Nowhere were there defences to ward off an entire fleet; partly because the need had not arisen, and partly because the increased range, accuracy and mobility of the cannon developed in the previous decades only now made such tactics possible. Plans were drawn up and work on building the forts started almost immediately.

Opposite left: *Charles V of Spain, the Holy Roman Emperor*. Opposite centre: *Francis I of France*. Opposite right: *Alessandro Farnese, Pope Paul III. (All British Museum)*. This page: *Catherine of Aragon (National Portrait Gallery)*.

7

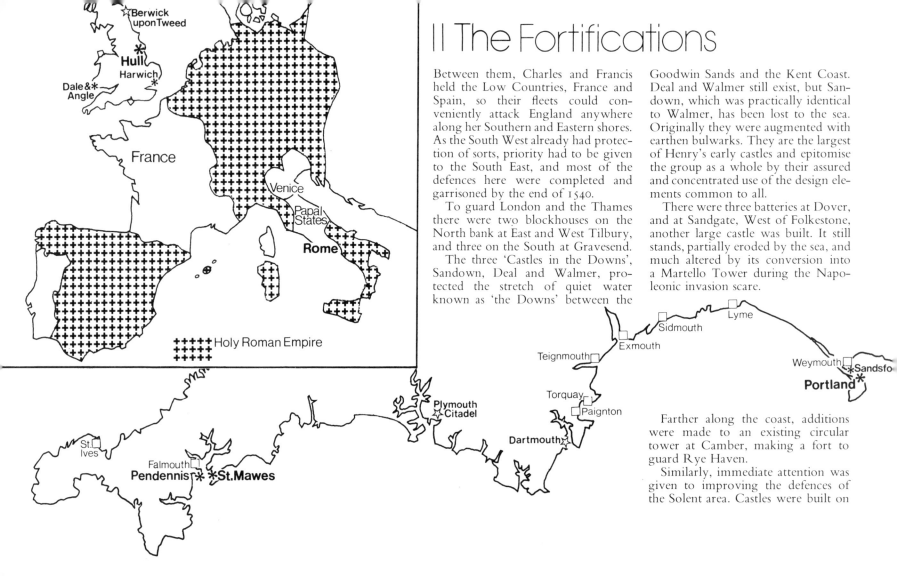

II The Fortifications

Between them, Charles and Francis held the Low Countries, France and Spain, so their fleets could conveniently attack England anywhere along her Southern and Eastern shores. As the South West already had protection of sorts, priority had to be given to the South East, and most of the defences here were completed and garrisoned by the end of 1540.

To guard London and the Thames there were two blockhouses on the North bank at East and West Tilbury, and three on the South at Gravesend.

The three 'Castles in the Downs', Sandown, Deal and Walmer, protected the stretch of quiet water known as 'the Downs' between the Goodwin Sands and the Kent Coast. Deal and Walmer still exist, but Sandown, which was practically identical to Walmer, has been lost to the sea. Originally they were augmented with earthen bulwarks. They are the largest of Henry's early castles and epitomise the group as a whole by their assured and concentrated use of the design elements common to all.

There were three batteries at Dover, and at Sandgate, West of Folkestone, another large castle was built. It still stands, partially eroded by the sea, and much altered by its conversion into a Martello Tower during the Napoleonic invasion scare.

Farther along the coast, additions were made to an existing circular tower at Camber, making a fort to guard Rye Haven.

Similarly, immediate attention was given to improving the defences of the Solent area. Castles were built on two shingle spits from the North shore, Calshot and Hurst, and two blockhouses were added at East and West Cowes, on the Isle of Wight. A report of 1539 explains how these four would command all normal approaches to Southampton Water.

Some small improvements were made to Portsmouth's defences, but West of the Solent area the only work known to have been complete and garrisoned by 1540 was Portland Castle, although Sandsfoot, its partner

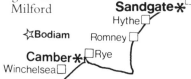

estuary he built two major forts, Pendennis and St. Mawes, as well as improving the blockhouses already there. He helped the town of Poole to build Brownsea Castle, and built blockhouses at Dale and Angle in Pembrokeshire to guard Milford Haven.

✳Henrician Castles
✲ Henrician Blockhouses
☆ Other Forts and Castles
▢ Towns

Left: *The Royal Arms at Pendennis Castle (Crown copyright).*

across Weymouth Harbour, may have been built simultaneously.

Thus the most urgent defences were completed with great speed. However, the alliance between Charles and Francis was proving very brittle and the fear of invasion lessened. But Henry persevered and continued the

line in both directions, though it must be admitted that the initial impetus was lost and the addition of the extra works took several years.

On the East Coast he initiated the construction of a castle linked to two blockhouses at Hull after a visit to the town in 1540. Likewise, blockhouses were built at Harwich.

In the West he started to add to the existing defences. To guard the Fal

Turning his attention to the Solent area again, he built Southsea Castle near Portsmouth, and made further improvements to the town defences there. Work was started on a major castle on the Isle of Wight at Sandown, and another was built at Yarmouth, at the instigation of Richard Worsley, who was Captain of the Island.

9

III The 1539/40 Castles

The individual works built in 1539–40, together with Pendennis and St. Mawes, share a number of characteristics that separate them from other defence works before or since. All are squat in form with thick walls accentuated by rounded parapets, the masses broken only by the wide splays of the gunports and embrasures. The main castles consist of a central circular keep or tower for gun-mounting and accommodation, surrounded by lower works housing further tiers of artillery. These additions usually take the form of round bastions attached directly to the keep, or more usually to a lower curtain wall or chemise around it. The blockhouses are often a simplification of this design consisting of a single platform of one or two storeys; a detached bastion, as it were, with or without accommodation for the gun crew behind. Everywhere one is impressed by their solidity and by the emphatically round shapes. If today we admire the symmetry and cleanness of line on aesthetic grounds, their purpose in the sixteenth century was entirely practical. The cylindrical bastions with their curved parapets

This page, above and top right: *Pendennis Castle.* Right: *Deal Castle from the north. The parapets were drastically altered in the eighteenth century. Hollar's view (Opposite) shows their original form (British Museum).*

10

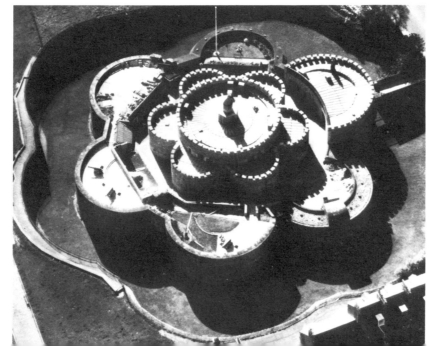

Deale Castle

Cales

The Needles

E AST VIEW of HURST CASTLE

Opposite & A:
*Hurst Castle, on
a shingle spit in the
Solent.* Top left &
B: *St Mawes Castle,
Cornwall.* Lower
left & C: *Walmer
Castle incorporates
the residence of the
Lord Warden of the
Cinque Ports.* Top
right & D: *Portland
Castle protected
Portland Bay.* (*All
Crown copyright*).

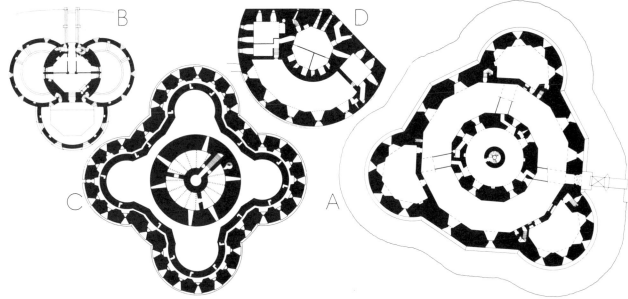

The typical rounded forms are clear in these pictures of St Mawes (above), Little Dennis (a waterline blockhouse which augments Pendennis Castle) (left), and Portland Castle (right) (Crown copyright).

14

were designed to withstand and deflect enemy shot. There are no unnecessary excrescences or sharp corners because these would be particularly vulnerable were the fort to come under fire. It is easy to forget the serious military purpose of many medieval castles whose great halls still seem to speak of pageantry and splendour. Not so with these castles: uncompromisingly they were fortresses, packing the maximum artillery capability into the most compact structures. Their dark interiors provided only the very minimum of living space for the Captain and his men. The Good Life had no place here. Henry had his palaces for that.

At most of them the sole decorative feature was a carved plaque over the entrance, normally carrying the Royal coat-of-arms. The only exceptions were Pendennis and St Mawes which boast such decorative flourishes as ornamental copings and window hoods, and grotesquely carved rainwater spouts. At St Mawes there was not one but several decorative plaques, as well as inscriptions running round the walls in praise of Henry and his son Edward, Duke of Cornwall. Not that any of these features were allowed to impair the military effectiveness.

Calshot Castle is sited at the mouth of Southampton Water. It was one of a number of castles and blockhouses designed to defend the anchorages north of the Isle of Wight (Crown copyright).

Interiors: original
timber partitions
survive at a number
of the castles. Above:
Carved lintel with a
loyal inscription at
St Mawes. Far
right: Portland, and
Deal, where the
staircase within a
central drum can also
be seen. Right: The
vaulted basement at
Deal. (All Crown
copyright)

Opposite: Walmer
Castle, as engraved
by Samuel and
Nathaniel Buck.

16

THE NORTH WEST VIEW OF WALMER CASTLE, IN THE COUNTY OF KENT.

To the R:t Hon:ble CHARLES Earl of *Middlesex* Son & Heir Apparent to the most Noble LIONEL Duke of *Dorset* This Prospect with all submission is Inscrib'd by his Lordships most Humble & most Obed:t Serv:ts Sam:l & Nath:l Buck.

THIS CASTLE standing on the Sea Shore, not far from Deal, was built in the times of K: Hen: VIII. Walmer was the Seat of the Noble Family of Criell from K: Hen: III time till K: Hen: V:s Reign when S:r Thomas Keriell or Criell dying without Issue Male one of his Daughters and Coheirs marrying S:r John Fogge Kn:t it came to him & by Anne one of the Daughters & Coheirs of S:r Tho:s Fogge Serj:t Porter of Calais it pass'd to Will: Scott Esq:r and next to Hen: Isham Esq:r whose Son Edw:d deceasing temp: Eliz: by Mary his sole Daughter & Heir it came to S:r Geo: Perkins Kn:t whose Daughter Mary by Marriage convey'd it to Richard Lord Minshull who A:D: 1627 sold it to James Hugesson of Linsted Esq:r in which Family it now remains. S: & N: Buck del: & fc: 1735.

St. Mawes:
Achievements of
arms, inscriptions,
figurehead gargoyles
and other decorative
devices.

IV Gunpower

Top centre: *A bombard*, Bottom centre: *A mortar & Centre page: Basilisks, all drawn early in the sixteenth century. (British Museum).*

The usefulness of all the forts relied largely on the power of the guns Henry was able to mount on them. The earliest guns in the fourteenth and fifteenth centuries had been either heavy bombards and mortars for attacking walls during sieges, or very light guns whose barrels were not cast but made of bars of metal bound together to form a tube. They were strapped to heavy base planks or fitted on elementary pivots. Many were breech-loaders; they were expensive to make, inefficient, and dangerous in the extreme. During the first decades of the sixteenth century improved methods of refining iron enabled such composite guns to be made a little more easily. Almost all cast guns were made of non-ferrous metals, usually

brass, as iron-working techniques were not advanced enough to produce sound castings. Henry followed developments closely. In 1518 he is reported to have visited Southampton and caused new guns 'to be fired again and again marking their range,' for he was 'very curious about matters of this kind.' At Calais fourteen years later, gunports were added to the fortifications there that were 'splaies which the Kinge's grace hath devised.' By this time cannon were conforming to a more or less regular range of sizes (saker, firing a 6 lb. shot; culverin 18

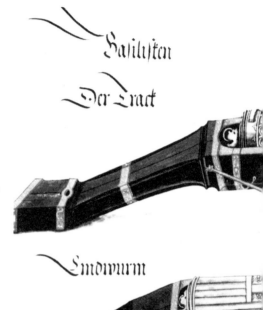

Basilisten

Der Tract

Smolwurm

Bottom left: *The use of guns during a siege, taken from a late fifteenth-century manuscript.*

lb. shot; basilisk 25 lb. shot; demi-cannon, 32 lb. shot). They could reach well over a mile, and were properly mounted on two-wheel, trailed carriages. Henry certainly had a great need for guns: field guns and bombards for his campaigns, and cannon for his warships and land defences. Hitherto he had bought guns abroad, mainly in the Low Countries, but during the thirties he had set up gun foundries in London and the Weald under the control of Continental gunfounders. Whether or not they were able to supply all the ordnance required to equip the new forts we do not know. Possibly not, for in

1543, Henry was arranging experiments to find a cheaper and quicker method of making cannon. He gathered together experts and craftsmen at an ironworks in Sussex, and finally their efforts were rewarded with a method of casting safe iron cannon.

Such then was the armament for which the castles were designed. The cannon were placed on top of the keep and both on and within the surrounding bastions. Since the individual guns had only a limited degree of vertical traverse, arranged in multiple tiers like this, they could cover a greater depth of field than would have been possible otherwise. Provided with carriages, horizontal traverse was less of a problem, but because of the great thickness of the walls, broad splays to the embrasures and gunports were essential. Where guns fired from enclosed lower storeys, they were placed in vaulted alcoves built into the thickness of the walls, termed casemates. Vents were provided in addition to the ports themselves to allow the gun smoke to disperse.

Though primarily sited to command a waterway, all the castles had provision for the artillery to fire inland; indeed the majority are quite symmetrical and no apparent prece-

dence is given to the seaward side in this respect. Used landwards, the fire would only be needed in a self-defensive role, to break up siege works or artillery positions. Great emphasis was laid on self-defence for much

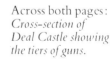

depended on these few castles and it was important that they should not fall to an advance enemy landing party. Every precaution was taken to ensure they could not be stormed. The castles were surrounded by a moat, usually dry, that could be raked with hand-gun fire from the lowest storey of the bastions. It was crossed by a drawbridge to an entrance incorporat-

Above: The *Pevensey Gun, Elizabethan; the carriage is a replica (Crown copyright).*

Across both pages: Cross-section of Deal Castle showing the tiers of guns.

23

*Deal Castle: Entry was carefully controlled by a series of barriers and was everywhere covered by positions of fire.
Below: The dry moat was raked by gunfire from both*

ing all the defensive paraphernalia developed in the Middle Ages: barred doors, portcullises, murder holes and so on. In the larger castles, entry was then through a gatehouse into the annular courtyard around the keep. This courtyard was also covered by handgun fire, either from the keep or from reversed positions in the outer

bastions. An attacker who had penetrated the main entrance could thus be prevented from reaching the door to the keep, invariably placed some way round. Full use was made of hand-guns. The normal type used was an arquebus: it was a form of elementary musket five or six feet long requiring a tripod stand and fired by

a matchlock. Better guns did exist: Henry had several wheel-lock pistols in his own collection. At the other extreme, bows and arrows were still part of the standard equipment of the forts.

Something is known of the garrison strengths. In 1540 one of the Thames batteries had a captain, deputy, porter,

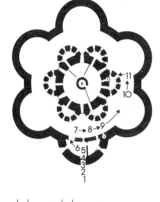

1

2

4

5

6

9

10

3

7

11

below and above. 1 The entrance to the castle beyond the drawbridge. 2 Above were 'murder holes' in the vault. 3 The iron-studded door. 4 The intruders were faced directly (5) by a cannon. 6 The way to the inner bailey was to the left but the shortest route to the entrance of the keep was to the right (7–11) covered by fire from all possible angles. (1–6 Peter Forster; 7–11 A. F. Kersting).

25

Hand-guns from Henry VIII's personal collection. They are probably German, made about 1537, and originally had wheel-lock mechanisms. Right: A hackbut man with matchlock gun.

Opposite: Sandown Castle, Kent, in the nineteenth century, before its destruction by the sea. (All Crown copyright).

two soldiers and six gunners. Deal had a captain and 34 others. A captain's pay varied between a shilling and two shillings a day. That of the deputy and porter was eightpence, and of a gunner sixpence. From this each man was expected to provide his own weapons: the gunners, for example, had to possess their own hand-gun. Within the masonry shell of a castle, the interior was mainly divided up by timber-framed partitions with wattle infill, although there were vaulted basements to the larger castles. A common allocation of space was for the upper floor of the keep to be used as lodgings for the captain and any officers; the basement would be for storage, leaving the ground floor for a common

mess hall, kitchens and soldiers' room. This was sometimes insufficient and the gunners had to use the outer bastions as sleeping quarters. At Camber even the kitchen is in a bastion, the flues of the bake-ovens sharing chimneys with the cannons' smoke vents.

The cost of building most of the castles is recorded. It varied from £500 for a small blockhouse to about £5000 for a medium-sized castle and £27,000 for the castles and bulwarks in the Downs. Much of the money was provided from the revenues seized from suppressed religious houses. For Sandgate a detailed day-to-day ledger book survives, giving particulars of all the money spent. From it a reasonably complete picture of the progress of the

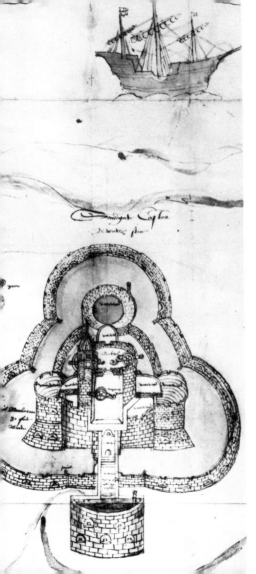

building operations can be drawn. In the spring of 1539 most of the workmen were occupied in constructing plant scaffolding, hods, barrows etc. Work began in earnest during the summer and the number of employees rose to a daily average of five hundred. Over the winter this number dropped to about one hundred, although by June 1540 it had risen again to six hundred and thirty. The work was completed by that autumn. Throughout there was a high proportion of skilled men: stone masons recruited in the West Country, bricklayers, carpenters and sawyers. They were paid sevenpence or eightpence a day. The labourers, who formed less than half the total, received fivepence. In the Downs the work force rose to well over a thousand. The work there did not pass without incident. In June 1539, nine men were sent to jail for leading a strike among the labourers in demand of an increase in pay. The Sandgate accounts shew that most of the stone used was local; Kentish ragstone in this case from the nearby cliffs. It was of poor quality and was heavily supplemented with Caen stone robbed from disused monasteries in the vicinity. Stone from similar sources can be identified at other castles of the scheme. Bricks and tiles were made at a dozen kilns as far away as Rye and Canterbury. Lime kilns and a forge were established, fired with local brushwood and coal from the North of England. Timber came from the Weald, and lead was obtained as further plunder from an abandoned priory. A whole host of ready-made goods were bought in from London, ranging from tents for the workmen to prefabricated wooden panelling.

Opposite: *Sandgate Castle, Kent, drawn in the eighteenth century (Kent County Records).*

This page, left: *Sandgate Castle, a sixteenth - century drawing (British Museum).* Centre: *Stone used in Yarmouth Castle, Isle of Wight, taken from a dissolved monastery.*

29

V The Development of Coastal Defence

Below: *Portchester Castle. The rectangular walls of the Roman Fort and, inside, on the left, the medieval castle (Aerofilms).* Right: *Catchcold Tower, Southampton, a*

Britain received its first system of coastal defence during the Roman Occupation, when a series of large forts at key points on the south-east coasts aided the 'Classis Britannica', the British Fleet. They were under the control of an officer called the 'Count of the Saxon Shore', the threat being mainly from raiders from Saxony.

After the Romans left there was not the political unity required to maintain the system, and until Henry's time coastal defence was always arranged in a somewhat piecemeal fashion. It had to be based on two things: a navy to ward off the enemy at sea, and adequately defended strong points on land (castles or towns) garrisoned to

provide troops to meet an invading army and prevent it marching far inland. Only rarely was either aspect solely the monarch's responsibility or solely the citizens'. For example, early in the Middle Ages the Cinque Ports were chartered. They provided the king with his navy in return for trading privileges. In later medieval times,

during the Hundred Years' War, many towns of the South rebuilt or strengthened their walls. But they relied to some extent on royal subsidies. Even individual landowners received encouragement from the king to build castles where these would contribute to the nation's defence.

Castle curtain or town wall, their tactical role was almost entirely self-defensive: to protect the ground inside and prevent entry by an enemy. The characteristic architectural features of medieval fortifications all served this purpose. The walls, for instance, were high, battlemented and machicolated, they were moated and were over-looked by projecting turrets, all to prevent them being scaled or undermined. When gunpowder and guns were introduced, in the fourteenth century, they had little influence on fortification design at first. Circular or 'inverted keyhole' shaped gunloops replaced slender arrow loops as guns joined the traditional weapons.

late-medieval town-wall defence with keyhole gunloops (National Monuments Record).

Below: *Bodiam Castle, Sussex, built under licence of 1385.*

Above: *Dartmouth Castle.* Opposite: *A sixteenth-century drawing of the Henrician blockhouse on Brownsea Island in Poole Harbour (British Museum).*

Gradually cannon became more fashionable, but they remained largely immobile and unreliable. It was not until the fifteenth century that the first fortifications were built in England to use artillery as their main armament and in an offensive capacity. One was Dartmouth Castle in Devon, built by the people of that town between 1481 and 1495, with aid from the king. Sited on the west bank of the River Dart, below the town, the guns fired from ports near water level. Although each was fixed to a heavy bed and could not be easily moved, together they covered the whole estuary, and no ship could pass by to the town unmarked. Tactically this was a great step forward, and many of the small blockhouses built along the West Country coast soon afterwards followed Dartmouth in purpose and design. However, in their proportions and in the strength of the structures themselves, they differed markedly from the blockhouses Henry was soon to build.

On the Continent the last decades of the fifteenth century and the first half of the sixteenth constituted a period of extensive experimentation in fortification design. The thin and lofty medieval town and castle walls were proving inadequate in the face of the concentrated pounding they could receive from siege artillery. More solidly built structures were essential. At the same time the possibility of using cannon to break up the besiegers' positions and keep them from the base of the walls was only now being fully appreciated. So throughout Europe, projecting gun towers and bastions, which could provide both forward and flanking fire, were added to town walls. They were squat circular or semi-circular structures with broad sloping or rounded parapets. The more sophisticated had an additional lower rank of guns, firing from smoke-vented casemates. In 1527 Albrecht Durer published a treatise on fortification in which he advocated the use of bastions such as these. Other suggestions he put into print were that an ideal fortress should have a keep surrounded by a bastioned curtain, and that moats could be covered by gunports at ground level. Thus Henry's castles were composed of elements all of which could have been found abroad at the time, either in practice or theory. What made them so distinctive was the unorthodox manner in which these components were assembled. Nowhere else had bastions been clustered so tightly together in such numbers, or had multiple tiers of gun positions been used to such effect. They were at once both more complex and more economical in design than their continental precursors.

Whose inspiration was this? One possibility is that the ideas were brought from Europe by a Bohemian, Stephen von Haschenperg. He is

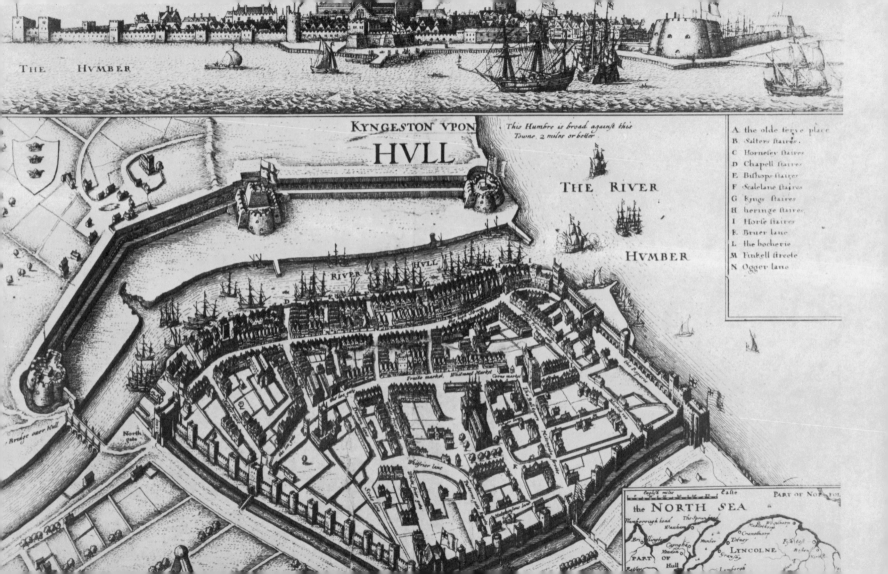

THE   HVMBER

KYNGESTON VPON

HVLL

This Humbre is broad against this
Towne, 2 miles or better

THE   RIVER

HVMBER

RIVER   HVLL

A. the olde terve place
B. Salters stayres.
C. Horneley stayres
D. Chapell stayres
E. Bishops stayres
F. Scalelane stayres
G. Kyngs stayres
H. heringe stayres
I. Horse stayres
K. Bruer lane
L. the bocherie
M. Finkell streete
N. Ogger lane

Bridge over Hull

North
Gate

the   NORTH SEA

PART OF NOR

English mile
PART OF Hull

LINCOLNE

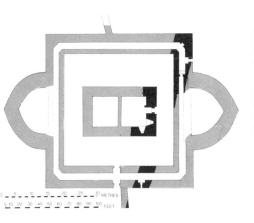

5 10 15 20 25 30 METRES
5 10 20 30 40 50 60 70 80 90 100 FEET

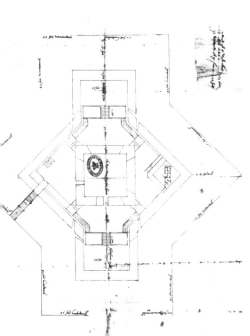

known to have 'devised' Sandgate and Camber Castles (at the former he also supervised the day to day building work), but it is not recorded who designed the others. It is possible that Henry himself played some part, for at the Downs and later at Southsea the 'device' is reported as being his. This may only be a courtesy afforded to him as king, but it must imply at least an especially close interest in the work.

With the exception of Pendennis and St. Mawes, the castles that Henry built from 1540 onwards demonstrate an interesting progression away from universally rounded forms. Their parapets were still curved in profile, but the ground plan became rectangular, and the bastions were no longer strictly cylindrical. At Hull the main castle of 1540 was centrally planned with a rectangular keep and surrounding chemise. There were two bastions, on opposite sides. Each had two curved faces closing to a point. Two trefoil-shaped blockhouses, each formed from three bastions of a similar type were connected to the castle by long walls. Almost identical blockhouses were recommended for the defences of Guisnes in the Pale of Calais in the same year. Southsea Cas-

tle, built in 1544, was similar in concept to Hull, but its bastions were triangular in plan. This abandonment of circular shapes seems to reflect a growing confidence in the strength of land-based artillery over the lesser guns of warships.

Two castles built in the 1540s on the Isle of Wight, Sandown and Yarmouth, had attached to one landward corner a straight-sided, pointed bastion with provision for guns to fire back along the faces of the adjacent main walls. At Yarmouth the gun-

Opposite: Seventeenth-century Hull, showing Henry VIII's defences (British Museum). This page left: Plan of Hull Castle as excavated.

Below, left: Southsea Castle in 1577 (Crown copyright). Below: Camber Castle.

Right: *The Elizabethan defences added to Carisbrooke Castle.*

Below: *Plan of Yarmouth Castle, Isle of Wight, which accompanied a survey of 1559 (Lord Dartmouth).*

ports were recessed behind the faces of the bastion and were thereby protected from enemy fire. Similar works were added to existing defences at Tynemouth Castle and Portsmouth at about the same time. These were the first examples in England of the 'Italian' style of bastion, which was to become the hallmark of a system of defence which lasted for three hundred years. These bastions could be spaced at intervals around a fortification, and guns sited in the flanks of one could give complete coverage across the long faces of its neighbours.

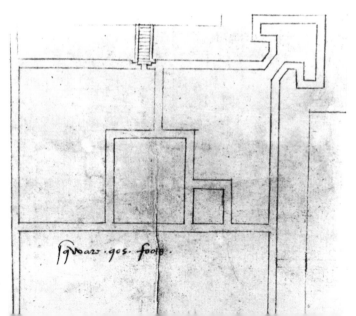

The plan had already been developed in Central Italy by 1500, but it was not until the 1540s that the advantages were appreciated elsewhere. Their use then spread rapidly across the whole of Europe. Simultaneously there was a gradual abandonment of masonry fortifications. They were replaced by broad ramparts built of earth to resist impact, and only revetted with stone or brick. The finest early example of the new style in Britain was in the series of Elizabethan works around Berwick-upon-Tweed begun in 1558. Others can be seen at Carisbrooke, in the Isle of Wight, and around Pendennis Castle.

By the seventeenth century the design of fortifications had become a science with many competing theorists publishing books on the subject. Among the most notable exponents were Vauban in France and Coehoorn in Holland. Broad moats and outworks of increasing complexity were enlarging defence works until they regularly occupied an area much greater than that which they enclosed. Firepower was meticulously arranged to ensure that an attacking force could

The remarkably
complete defences
around Berwick-
upon-Tweed.
Building started in
Mary I's reign and
continued in
Elizabeth's. Guns
were mounted on top
of the earth-filled
bastions as well as in
the recessed positions
on their flanks
(Aerofilms).

37

Tilbury Fort: Air photograph from the west, and one of Sir Bernard de Gomme's plans of the fort, drawn in 1670. It remains very little altered, except in the south-east, where a nineteenth-century battery replaced the bastion (British Museum).

Opposite: Pendennis Castle, a Buck print of 1734 (Crown copyright).

not breach any of the lines of defence without remaining continuously under the defenders' fire. In England fear of increasing Dutch naval power in Charles II's reign led him to employ a Dutch-born engineer, Sir Bernard de Gomme, to design and execute a number of coastal defence works. The most important were at Plymouth and Portsmouth, and on the Thames and Medway. Tilbury Fort in Essex and Plymouth Citadel remain as visible reminders of the magnitude of the works of the period.

The eighteenth century saw sporadic improvements and alterations made to existing defence works as ideas changed. They were never great as the underlying principles of the bastioned system were firmly adhered to. These principles were not challenged until the very end of the eighteenth

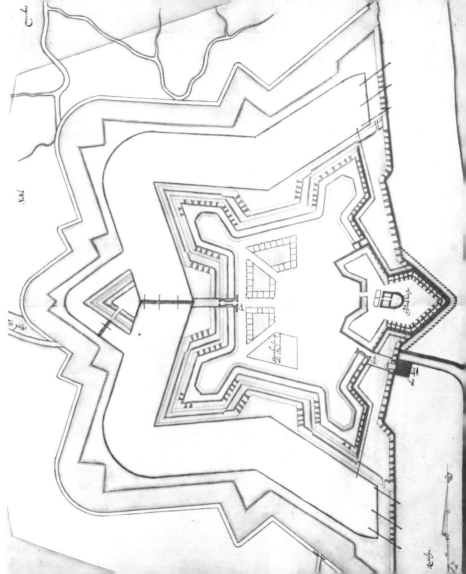

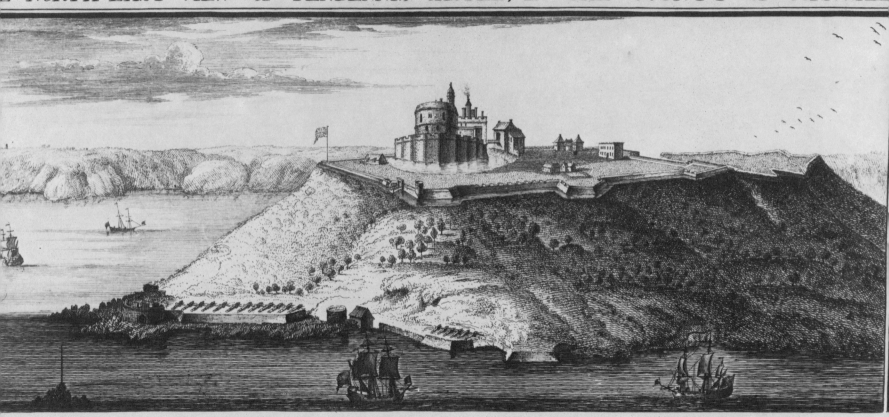

HIS CASTLE of Pendennis or Pendinas, stands on a Peninsula; it is large and well fortify'd, built by K. Hen:8.th for the Defence of Falmouth Harbour. Q. Eliz added considerably to the Fortifications. It held out a-long Time for K. Cha:1.st but after a Strait Seige, it was forced to Surrender to the Parliament Forces.

S. & N: Buck delin. et sculp. 17

THE EAST VIEW OF St. MAWS CASTLE, IN THE COUNTY OF CORNWALL.

To Mrs ANNE KNIGHT Relict of John Knight of
Gosfield Bell House in the County of Essex Esqr. & Lady of the Manour
of St. Maw's in the County of Cornwall.
This Prospect is humbly Inscrib'd by
her very humble Servts.
Samel. & Nathl. Buck.

THIS CASTLE receives its Name of St. Mawds or St. Mawdits from
the adjoyning Town. It is on the East side of Falmouth Harbour,
Pendennis is on the West side, and was built by K. Hen: VIII at ye same
time with that, and for ye same purpose: that is for ye Defence of ye Harb

1. Pendennis Castle   3. Penreen   5. Flushing
2. Falmouth   4. Worth Esqr. Seat 6. Trefusis Esqr. Seat

J. & N. Buck. del. et

century and were not abandoned until the nineteenth. In the first few years of that century fear of invasion by Napoleon led to the siting of many small batteries at ports and harbours, and to the building of the so-called, Martello Towers (seventy-four of them) to guard low-lying shores in the South East.

Fifty years later another Napoleon, Louis, seemed set to repeat his uncle's conquest of Europe. England felt particularly threatened, and particularly unsure of her defences. By now the bastioned fortifications were wholly discredited as too passive for warfare with the latest more powerful artillery. A Royal Commission was set up, and following its recommendations to refortify selected areas (Thames, Medway, Solent, Plymouth, Milford Haven), a grander programme of fort building was embarked upon than England had ever seen. The most impressive parts of this scheme were the rings of huge forts built around Portsmouth and Plymouth. These were examples of the new 'polygonal system'. Each fortress contained its own barracks and was heavily armed with powerful guns in bomb-proof casemates. The aim was to use these guns to their maximum advantage and

cover as great an area of land and sea as was possible, thus preventing an enemy approaching the towns in question. For the first time since Henry built his forts, purely self-defensive arrangements were strictly separate, consisting in the main of dry moats covered by small arms fire from projecting bomb-proof galleries.

These were the last self-contained and self-defensible fortresses. The drastic changes in warfare of the last hundred years have made them obsolete. The coastal defences of the

Second World War consisted of almost continuous barricading, supported by many hundreds of small batteries and gun emplacements, and by cover from the air.

None of the major coastal defence systems has ever been thoroughly tested in action. It was said of the 1860 Commission defences: 'The object of the fortifications is not so much to resist as to deter'. In this respect our coastal defences have always served their purpose.

Opposite: *St Mawes Castle, a Buck print of 1734 (Crown copyright)*.

Below: *Fort Nelson, one of the 1860 Royal Commission forts ringing Portsmouth (Aerofilms)*.

VI Open to the Public

Hours of admission to Monuments in the care of the Department of the Environment (subject to revision at any time). *A:* At any reasonable hour. *S:* Standard Hours: weekdays 9.30 am to 7 pm (May–September), to 5.30 pm (March, April and October) and to 4 pm (November–February). Sundays open at 2 pm except for *SM:* from 9.30 am (April–September). All monuments are closed from Christmas Eve to Boxing Day and on New Year's Day. Some smaller monuments may close for a lunch hour, normally 1–2 pm.

COASTAL DEFENCE WORKS IN THE CARE OF THE DEPARTMENT OF THE ENVIRONMENT

Burgh Castle, Norfolk, *S.* **Bayard's Cove Castle,** Dartmouth, Devon, *A.* **Calshot Castle,** Hampshire, and **Camber Castle,** East Sussex–not yet open. **Carisbrooke Castle,** Isle of Wight, *S.* **Dartmouth Castle,** Devon, *S SM.* **Deal Castle,** Kent, *S SM.* **Dymchurch, Martello Tower No 24,** Kent, *S SM* April–September only. **Fort Brockhurst,** Hampshire, not yet open. **Hurst Castle,** Hampshire *S SM.* **Isles of Scilly: The Garrison Walls, Harry's Walls, King Charles's Cas-** tle and Cromwell's Castle, *A.* **Pendennis Castle,** Cornwall, *S SM.* **Pevensey Castle,** East Sussex, *S SM.* **Plymouth Citadel,** *A*, but at the discretion of the Military. **Portchester Castle,** Hampshire, *S SM.* **Portland Castle,** Dorset, *S* April–September only. **Reculver Roman Fort,** Kent, *A.* **Richborough Castle,** Kent, *S SM.* **St Catherine's Castle,** Fowey, Cornwall, 9 am to sunset. **St Mawes Castle,** Cornwall, *S SM.* **Tilbury Fort,** Essex, *S.* **Upnor Castle,** Kent, *S.* **Walmer Castle,** Kent, *S SM*, but closed on Mondays (except Bank Holidays), and when the Lord Warden is in residence. **Yarmouth Castle,** Isle of Wight, *S.*

COASTAL DEFENCE WORKS IN PRIVATE OR MUNICIPAL OWNERSHIP

Berry Head Fortifications, Torbay, Devon. **Bodiam Castle,** East Sussex. **Eastbourne Martello Tower (Wish Tower),** East Sussex. **Great Yarmouth Town Walls,** Norfolk. **Herstmonceux Castle,** East Sussex. **King's Lynn Town Walls,** Norfolk, consist- ing of Southgate and various other sections of the wall scattered throughout the town. **Polruan Blockhouse,** Cornwall, on the opposite bank of River Fowey to the town of Fowey. **Portsmouth Defences,** Hampshire: Fort Wigley, Point Battery, Round Tower. **Sandsfoot Castle,** Weymouth, Dorset. **Southampton Town Walls,** Hampshire. **Southsea Castle,** Hampshire.